UPDATED EDITION

Guess What!

Student's Book 4
with eBook

American English

Susannah Reed with Kay Bentley

Series Editor: Lesley Koustaff

CAMBRIDGE

Contents

Welcome back!

Look!

Guess What!

1 🎧 0.01 **Listen and point.**

2 🎧 0.02 **Listen, point, and repeat.**

Lucas

Lily

Max

Tom

Anna

3 🎧 0.03 **Listen and say the names.**

4 (Think) **Describe and guess who.**

Is it a girl or a boy?   It's a boy.

Does he have dark hair?   No, he doesn't.

Is it Tom?   Yes, it is.

❶ dark hair
❷ straight hair
❸ glasses
❹ fair hair
❺ curly hair
❻ red hair

5 🎧 0.04 Listen and match. Then sing the song.

1 What does Fred look like?
He's tall, he has blue eyes,
And he has red hair.
He has short red hair.

2 What does Jane look like?
She's tall, she has brown eyes,
And she has straight hair.
She has long straight hair.

3 What does Paul look like?
He's short, he has brown eyes,
And he has dark hair.
He has short dark hair.

6 Look at page 6. Read and match.

1 What does Lucas look like?

a She's tall. She has long straight hair.

2 What does Lily look like?

b He's short. He has brown eyes.

3 What does Tom's sister look like?

c He's tall. He has short fair hair.

4 What does Anna's brother look like?

d She's short. She has red hair.

7 (About Me) Think about your family. Ask and answer.

What does your cousin look like?

She's short, and she has straight dark hair.

Remember!

What does he look like?
He's tall.
He has blue eyes.

Grammar fun!

8 🎧 0.05 **Listen and repeat.**

100 cm = 1 m

10 cm   20 cm   30 cm   40 cm   50 cm   60 cm   70 cm   80 cm   90 cm   100 cm

9 🎧 0.06 **Listen and match. Then ask and answer with a friend.**

a 76 cm

b 1 m, 32 cm

c 91 cm

d 1 m, 67 cm

e 1 m, 19 cm

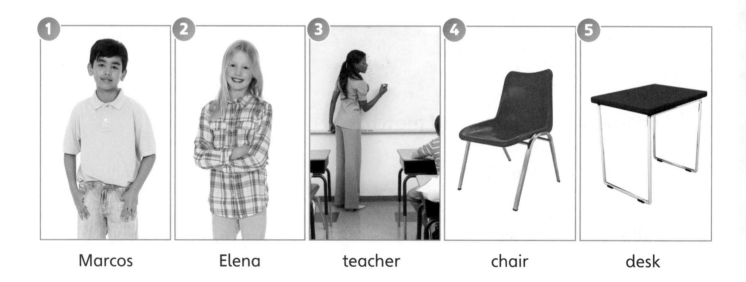

1 Marcos   2 Elena   3 teacher   4 chair   5 desk

How tall is Marcos?   He's 1 meter, 32 centimeters.

How high is the chair?   It's 91 centimeters.

10 About Me **Measure your friends. Then ask and answer.**

How tall are you?   I'm 1 meter, 25 centimeters.

Remember!

100 centimeters = 1 meter

11 🎧 0.07 **Go to page 102. Listen and repeat the chant.**

Grammar fun!

Grammar
→ Workbook page 6

Skills: *Reading and speaking*

 What activities do you do with your friends?

12 🎧 0.08 **Read and listen. Then match.**

My friends

1 My best friend's name is Rosa. She's very tall. She's 1 meter, 36 centimeters! She has long dark hair, and brown eyes. We like music, and we like playing the recorder together. We have recorder lessons every Wednesday.

2 This is my friend Louis. He has straight dark hair, and green eyes. We're in the same class at school. We like playing Ping-Pong. We play after school on Wednesdays. We like badminton, too.

c

a

b

3 This is me with my friends Sally and James. We like horseback riding. We have riding lessons on Sundays, and we like taking care of the horses, too. Horses are my favorite animals. They're beautiful.

13 **Read again and answer the questions.**

1 How tall is Rosa?
2 Does Rosa have recorder lessons on Sundays?
3 What does Louis look like?
4 What day do Sally and James go horseback riding?

14 (About Me) **Think of a friend and answer the questions.**

What's his or her name?
What does he or she look like?
Do you like the same things?
What activities do you do together?

Writing

→ Workbook page 7: Write about a friend and what he or she likes doing.

1. What should we do this afternoon?
   How about swimming?
   No, let's watch TV.

2. Look! It's *Daisy does it!*
   Great! That's my favorite TV program!

3. Do you want to help your local community?
   I do! I do!
   Anna! Sit down.

4. We're making a new Adventure Playground. Register online for the free app.
   Exciting! Let's register now!

5. What should we call our team?
   How about the Adventurers? We all like adventures.
   Good idea.

   Adventure Playground
   Eight weeks to make an Adventure Playground
   Registration Form   Team name
   name Lucas name Lily name Tom name Anna
   age 10 age 11 age 12 age 5
   Parental permission obtained ☑

6. Adventure Playground
   Welcome, Adventurers!
   Look for a challenge every week.
   See you soon!

16   **Listen and repeat. Then act.**

watching TV   going ice-skating   making models
playing the guitar   going bowling   playing Ping-Pong

1

What should we do today?

How about watching TV?

OK.

2

What should we do today?

How about playing the guitar?

No, let's go fishing.

OK, good idea.

Say it!

17 **Listen and repeat.**

Owls make no sound when they fly down.

owl

What **patterns** can you **see?**

1 🎧 0.12 Listen and repeat.

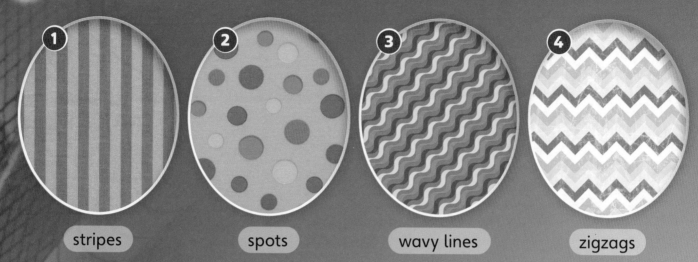

1 stripes

2 spots

3 wavy lines

4 zigzags

2 CLIL ▶ Watch the video.

3 What patterns can you see in the pictures?

Guess What! We all have different patterns of wavy lines on our fingers.

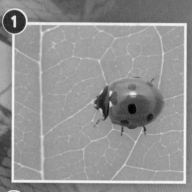

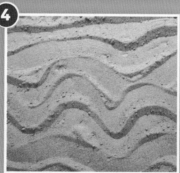

Let's collaborate!

famous   research

discuss   OUR MAGAZINE INTERVIEW   choose

interview

write

4 What patterns do you like drawing?

1 Fun sports

Look!

Guess What!

1 🎧 1.01 **Listen and point.**

2 🎧 1.02 **Listen, point, and repeat.**

Adventure vacations

1 fishing
2 ice-skating
3 skateboarding
4 sailing
5 kayaking
6 bowling
7 mountain biking
8 skiing
9 snowboarding

3 🎧 1.03 **Listen and answer the questions.**

4 (About Me) **Ask and answer with a friend.**

Do you like skiing?   Yes, I do.

5 (1.04) **Listen and choose. Then sing the song.**

1 I'm good at ice-skating/mountain biking,
But I'm not very good at skiing.
Sally isn't good at ice-skating/mountain biking,
But she's very good at skiing.
Sally's a good friend,
But we're good at different things.
Yes! Sally's a good friend,
But we're good at different things.

2 I'm good at snowboarding/skateboarding,
But I'm not very good at sailing.
Ricky isn't good at snowboarding/
skateboarding,
But he's very good at sailing.
Ricky's a good friend,
But we're good at different things.
Yes! Ricky's a good friend,
But we're good at different things.

6 (About Me) **Make sentences about you and your friends. Say _true_ or _false_.**

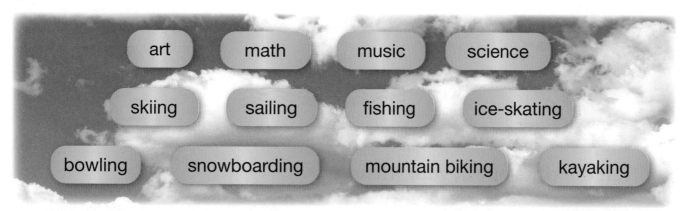

art   math   music   science

skiing   sailing   fishing   ice-skating

bowling   snowboarding   mountain biking   kayaking

I'm good at bowling.   True!

Juan isn't very good at ice-skating.   False!

Remember!

She's very good at skiing.
I'm not very good at sailing.

Grammar fun!

→ Workbook page 13   Grammar   17

7 🎧 1.05 **Listen and repeat.**

1 Are you good at skiing?
Yes, I am.
No, I'm not.

2 What are you good at?
I'm good at ice-skating.

8 (Think) **Look and choose. Then ask and answer with a friend.**

9 **Tell the class about your friend.**

Matthew is good at playing Ping-Pong.

Remember

Are you good at playing the guitar?
Yes, I am.   No, I'm not.
What are you good at?
I'm good at making movies.

10 🎧 1.06 **Go to page 102. Listen and repeat the chant.**

Grammar fun!

Grammar

→ Workbook page 14

Skills: *Listening and speaking*

Let's start! **Do you like talent shows?**

11 🎧 1.07 **Listen and match.**

Forest School Talent Show!
4:30 this afternoon in the school auditorium.

1 Mel   **2** Kim   **3** Alex

a   **b**   **c**

12 🎧 1.07 **Listen again and answer the questions.**

1 How old is Mel?
2 Is Kim good at making movies?
3 Can Alex play the piano?
4 Who is the winner of the talent show?

13 (About Me) **Plan a talent show with your friends.**

What are you good at?

I'm good at music. I can play the piano.

I can sing!

Writing

→ Workbook page 15: Plan a talent show.

🎧 1.08 ▶ Story **Read and listen. Watch.**

Value: Allow others to work

→ Workbook page 16

15   **Listen and repeat. Then act.**

| wash the car | paint a picture | make a movie |
| write a story | make a cake | sing a song |

1

Who wants to make a cake?

I do. I'm good at making cakes.

2

Who wants to paint a picture?

I don't. I'm not good at art.

Say it!

16 **Listen and repeat.**

Royal pythons coil into balls on the soil.

royal python

What kind of body movements can we make?

1 🎧 1.11 Listen and repeat.

turn   shake   bend   stretch   kick

2 CLIL ▶ Watch the video.

3 What body movements are the children making in these pictures?

Guess What!
We all make the same body movement when we're happy. We smile.

Let's collaborate!

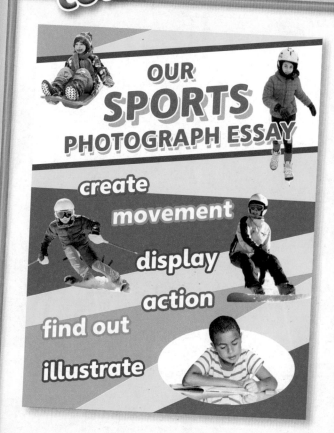

OUR SPORTS PHOTOGRAPH ESSAY

create
movement
display
action
find out
illustrate

4 What body movements do you make in sports?

→ Workbook page 18   CLIL: Physical education   23

2 Around town

Look!

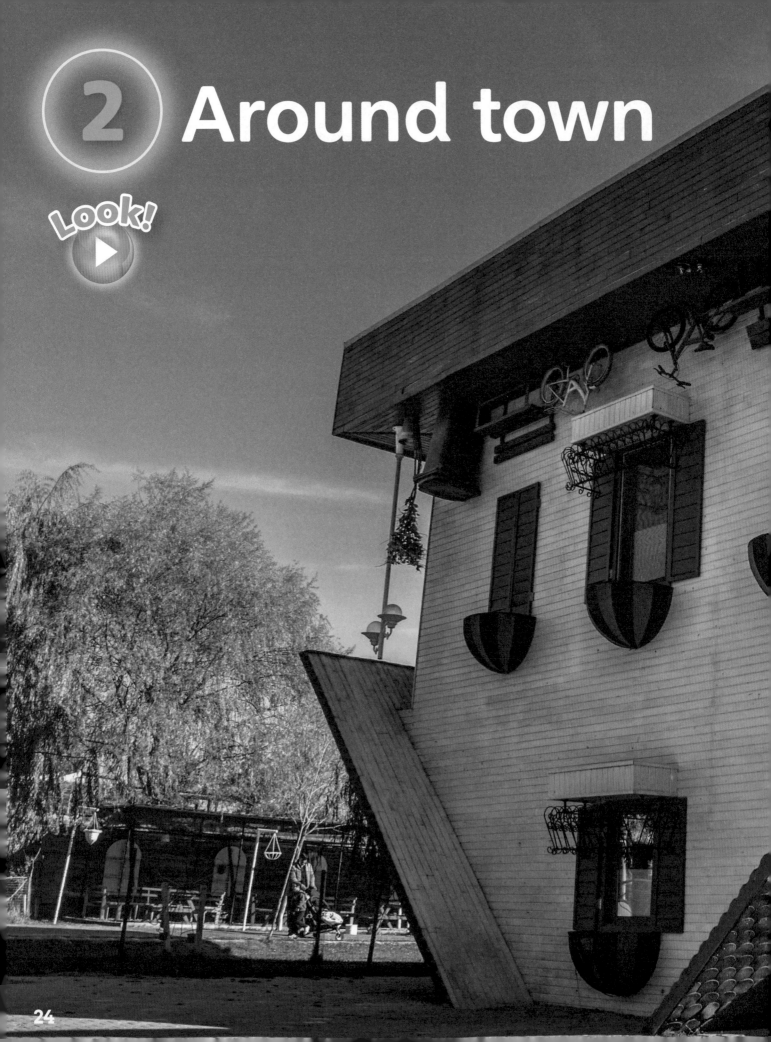

Guess What!

1 🎧 2.01 **Listen and point.**

2 🎧 2.02 **Listen, point, and repeat.**

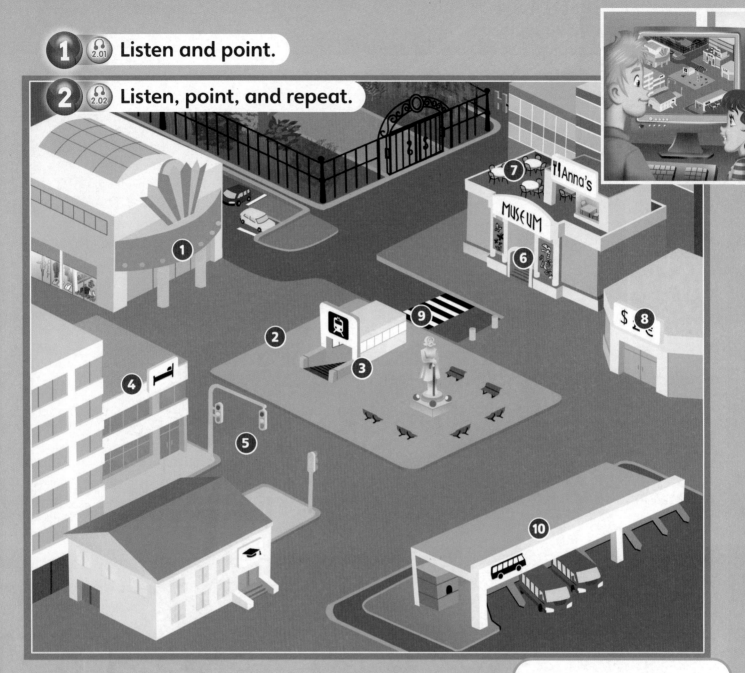

3 🎧 2.03 **Listen and say the words.**

4 Think **Look at Tom's map. Describe and guess where.**

It's across from the park.   Museum!

❶ shopping mall
❷ square
❸ subway station
❹ hotel
❺ traffic light
❻ museum
❼ restaurant
❽ bank
❾ crosswalk
❿ bus station

5 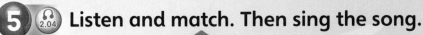 🎧 2.04 **Listen and match. Then sing the song.**

1 Where's the museum?
It's in the square.
It's across from the hotel.
Can you see it over there?

2 Where's the subway station?
It's below the square.
It's close to the shopping mall.
Can you see it over there?

3 Where's the plane?
It's above the square.
It's far from the town.
Can you see it up there?

6 **Read and match.**

1 Where's the museum?

2 Where's the plane?

3 Where's the shopping mall?

4 Where's the subway station?

a It's close to the subway station.

b It's below the square.

c It's above the square.

d It's across from the hotel.

7 (About Me) **Make a map of your town. Then ask and answer.**

Where's the bank?

It's across from the school.

No, it isn't! It's next to the museum!

Remember

Where's the bus station?
It's far from the hotel.

Grammar fun!

8 **Listen and repeat.**

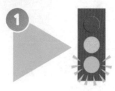

1 Start!

2 Go straight ahead.

3 Turn left.

4 Turn right.

5 Stop!

9 **Listen and follow. Then answer.**

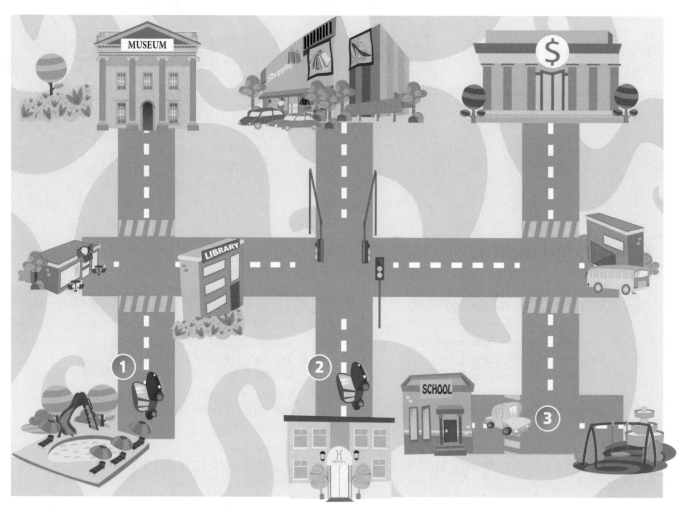

10 **Play the game with a friend.**

Start at the restaurant.   Turn left at the crosswalk.

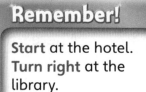
Remember!
Start at the hotel.
Turn right at the library.

11 **Go to page 102. Listen and repeat the chant.**

Grammar

→ Workbook page 22

Skills: *Reading and speaking*

 What can you see in your town?

12 🎧 2.08 **Read and listen. Then match.**

My trip to London!

Morning ¹ This is London Zoo. It's really big. It's close to my hotel. There are lots of animals in the zoo. This is the giraffe house. Giraffes are my favorite animal.

Lunch ² This is the Rain Forest Café. It's my favorite restaurant in London. What can you see behind the tables? They're elephants!

Afternoon ³ This is the Science Museum. And this is my favorite room – the transportation area. There are lots of cars and a truck. And look above the people. There's a plane!

Evening ⁴ This is Trafalgar Square. There's a big art gallery here. There are statues and a fountain, too.

13 **Read again and choose the words.**

1 London Zoo is close to/far from his hotel.
2 The Rain Forest Café is his favorite shopping mall/restaurant.
3 There's a plane above/below the people in the Science Museum.
4 There's a big art gallery/bus station in Trafalgar Square.

14 (About Me) **Ask and answer with a friend.**

What's your favorite city?
What can you see there?

Writing

→ Workbook page 23: Write about your favorite city.

Value: Cycle safely → Workbook page 24

16   **Listen and repeat. Then act.**

> library   sports field   shopping mall
> supermarket   bus station   museum

1

Excuse me. How do you get to the **bus station**?

Turn left at the crosswalk and go straight ahead.

Thank you.

2

Excuse me. How do you get to the **shopping mall**?

Turn right at the traffic lights and go straight ahead.

Thank you.

Say it!

17 🎧 2.11 **Listen and repeat.**

Turtles whirl in the surf.

What **3-D shapes** can you see?

1 🎧 2.12 **Listen and repeat.**

1	2	3	4	5
sphere	cylinder	cone	cube	pyramid

2 CLIL ▶ **Watch the video.**

3 **What shapes can you see? Read and match.**

1 This building is a pyramid shape with glass squares.
2 This building is a cube shape.
3 This building has cylinders at the front.
4 This building is a cone shape.
5 This building has a glass sphere on top.

Guess What!
Some Mexican pyramids are 3,000 years old, but some Egyptian pyramids are 4,000 years old.

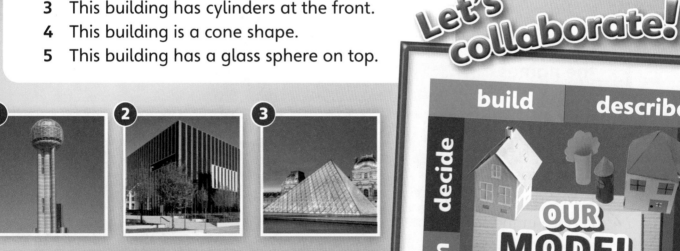

Let's collaborate!

build   describe
decide   design
brainstorm   compare

OUR MODEL TOWN

4 **What shapes can you see in buildings close to your school?**

Review Units 1 and 2

Fred

Alice

Josh

Mia

1 Find the words in the puzzles and match to the photographs.

fis

boarding

skate

hing

kaya

arding

snowbo

king

2 🎧 2.13 Listen and say the names.

3 Answer the questions.

1 Where's Fred?
2 What's Josh good at?
3 Is Mia good at skiing?
4 Is Alice in the square?

4 Make your own word puzzles for your friend.

Choose activities
or places in town:
super   urant
resta   market

34

→ Workbook pages 28–29

5 Play the game.

	A	B	C	D
1				
2				
3				
4				

Red

Are you good at (skateboarding)?

Blue

What does he/she look like?

Green

Where's the (bus station)?

Number 1. Letter A.   Are you good at skateboarding?   Yes, I am.

35

Look!

Guess What!

1 🎧 3.01 **Listen and point.**

2 🎧 3.02 **Listen, point, and repeat.**

What do people do?

3 🎧 3.03 **Listen and say the words.**

4 Think **Describe and guess who.**

She likes helping people.
She's wearing a white coat.

Doctor!

❶ doctor
❷ nurse
❸ artist
❹ singer
❺ actor
❻ vet
❼ businessman
❽ businesswoman
❾ bus driver
❿ pilot

5 🎧 3.04 Listen and choose. Then sing the song.

1 What does your aunt do? …
She's an artist/singer.
Where does she work? …
She works in a studio.

2 What does your uncle do? …
He's a bus driver/pilot.
Where does he work? …
He works on a plane.

3 What does your cousin do? …
She's a businesswoman/doctor.
Where does she work? …
She works in an office.

6 Read and match.

 a
 b
 c
 d

1 My dad's a farmer. He works on a farm.

2 My grandma's a teacher. She works in a school.

3 My mom's a train driver. She works on a train.

4 My grandpa's a doctor. He works in a hospital.

7 (About Me) Think about your family. Ask and answer.

What does your cousin do?

He's a nurse.

Where does he work?

He works in a hospital.

Remember!

What does your aunt do?
She's an artist.
Where does she work?
She works in a studio.

8 🎧 3.05 Listen and repeat.

1
What do you want to be?

I want to be a soccer player.

2
Do you want to be a soccer player?

No, I don't. I want to be a singer.

9 About Me Choose what you want to be. Then ask and answer.

10 Tell the class about your friend.

Sally wants to be an actor.

11 🎧 3.06 Go to page 102. Listen and repeat the chant.

→ Workbook page 32

Remember

What do you want to be?
I want to be a teacher.

Grammar fun!

Grammar

Skills: *Listening and speaking*

Let's start! **Where do you want to work?**

12 (3.07) **Listen and match.**

a

b

Sanjay

c

d

Lola

13 (3.07) **Listen again and say *true* or *false*.**

1 Sanjay's good at science.
2 Sanjay wants to be a doctor.
3 Lola wants to work in an office.
4 Lola's good at English.

14 (About Me) **Ask and answer with a friend.**

What are you good at?
Do you want to work with animals or people?
Do you want to work in a school or in an office?

Writing

 Workbook page 33: Write about what you want to be and where you want to work.

Value: Take care of pets and animals

→ Workbook page 34

16   **Listen and repeat. Then act.**

give some water to the horse   feed the rabbit   feed the cat
give some milk to the cat   take the dog for a walk

1
Should I take the dog for a walk?
Yes, please.

2
Should I feed the cat?
No, thanks. But you can feed the rabbit.
OK.

Say it!

17 **Listen and repeat.**

Crabs crawl across sand.

crab

What kind of
work
is it?

44

1 🎧 3.11 Listen and repeat.

outdoor work

factory work

transportation work

store work

2 CLIL ▶ Watch the video.

3 Look at the pictures. What kind of work can you see?

Guess! What?
We know how old a tree is from the number of circles in its wood.

4 What kinds of work do you think are difficult?

Let's collaborate!

discuss OUR choose
DREAM JOBS FAIR
write
research roleplay
ask and answer

Look!

Guess What!

1 🎧 4.01 **Listen and point.**

2 🎧 4.02 **Listen, point, and repeat.**

3 🎧 4.03 **Listen and say the animals.**

4 Think **Describe and guess what.**

It's brown, and it can jump. It has a long tail.

Kangaroo!

1 kangaroo
2 koala
3 parrot
4 penguin
5 bat
6 owl
7 jaguar
8 bear
9 panda
10 gorilla

5 (4.04) **Listen and match. Then sing the song.**

1 Gorillas are bigger than pandas,
But gorillas are smaller than bears.
Bears are bigger than gorillas,
And they're bigger than pandas, too.
Animals, animals. Look at the animals!

2 Bats are noisier than koalas,
But bats are quieter than parrots.
Parrots are noisier than bats,
And they're noisier than koalas, too.
Animals, animals. Look at the animals!

6 **Read and say *true* or *false*.**

1 Pandas are smaller than bears.
2 Gorillas are bigger than bears.
3 Bears are bigger than pandas.
4 Bats are noisier than parrots.
5 Koalas are quieter than bats.
6 Parrots are quieter than koalas.

7 (About Me) **Make sentences about your favorite animals. Say *true* or *false*.**

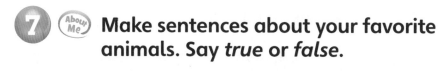

Tigers are faster than rabbits.

True!

Remember

bigger
smaller
noisier
quieter

Grammar fun!

8 🎧 4.05 **Listen and repeat.**

1 Are giraffes taller than penguins?

Yes, they are.

2 Are koalas noisier than bears?

No, they aren't.

9 🎧 4.06 **Listen and answer the questions.**

1 small / big

2 tall / short

3 noisy / quiet

4 slow / fast

10 Think **Ask and answer with a friend.**

Are frogs bigger than penguins?   No, they aren't.

11 🎧 4.07 **Go to page 102. Listen and repeat the chant.**

Remember!

Are parrots quieter than rabbits?
Yes, they are.   No, they aren't.

Grammar fun!

Grammar

→ Workbook page 40

Skills: *Reading and speaking*

Let's start! **Would you like to work in a zoo?**

12 🎧 4.08 **Read and listen. Then match.**

a

b

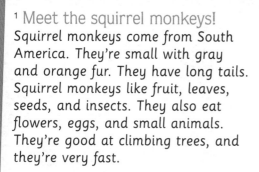

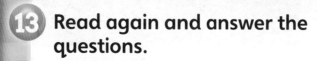
c

¹ Meet the squirrel monkeys!
Squirrel monkeys come from South America. They're small with gray and orange fur. They have long tails. Squirrel monkeys like fruit, leaves, seeds, and insects. They also eat flowers, eggs, and small animals. They're good at climbing trees, and they're very fast.

² Meet the wallabies!
A wallaby looks like a kangaroo, but it's smaller. Wallabies come from Australia. They eat grass and plants. Wallabies can't run, but they're very good at jumping.

³ Meet our baby red panda!
This is Bo. He's our baby red panda! Red pandas come from Asia. They're red and brown, and they have long tails. Red pandas eat lots of things. They like plants, insects, eggs, birds, and small animals!

13 **Read again and answer the questions.**

1 Can squirrel monkeys climb trees?
2 What do wallabies eat?
3 Do red pandas eat meat?
4 Which animal comes from Australia?

14 (About Me) **Ask and answer with a friend.**

What's your favorite wild animal?
What does it look like?
Where does it come from?
What does it eat?

Writing

➡ Workbook page 41: Write about your favorite animal.

15 4.09 Story ▶ **Read and listen. Watch.**

16   **Listen and repeat. Then act.**

kite   eraser   glue   balls   colored markers   scissors

1

Where's the glue?

It's here.

Can you pass it, please?

Yes, of course.

2

Where are the scissors?

They're here.

Can you pass them, please?

Yes, of course.

Say it!

17  **Listen and repeat.**

Frogs catch fruit flies with their tongues.

frog

What animal group is it?

1 🎧 4.12 **Listen and repeat.**

mammals

reptiles

amphibians

2 CLIL ▶ **Watch the video.**

Guess What!
The hummingbird is the only bird that can fly backward.

3 **What animal group is it? Read and match.**

1 It's an amphibian. It can live on land and in water.
2 It's a bird, and it can fly.
3 It's a fish, and it can swim.
4 It's a mammal. It has spots on it, and it can climb.
5 It's a reptile, and it can walk and swim.

Let's Collaborate!

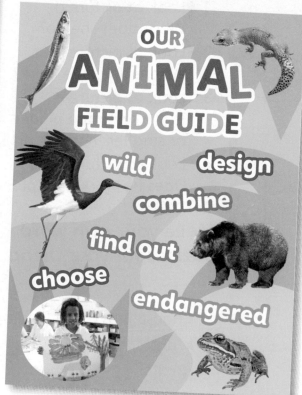

OUR **ANIMAL** FIELD GUIDE

wild   design
      combine
   find out
choose
      endangered

4 **What group of animals would you like to film?**

Review Units 3 and 4

1 Find the words in the puzzles and match to the photographs.

v*t

p*l*t

s*ng*r

*rt*st

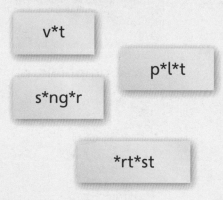

2 🎧 4.13 Listen and say the letters.

3 Read and answer the questions.

1 Look at picture a. What does she do?
2 Look at picture b. Where does she work?
3 Look at picture c. Is the sculpture bigger or smaller than the artist?
4 Look at picture d. Does he work on a plane?

4 Make your own word puzzles for your friend.

Choose jobs or wild animals:

k*ng*r**

g*r*ll*

→ Workbook pages 46–47

5 Play the game.

Red
Do you want to be a (doctor)?

Blue
Does (a farmer) work in (an office)?

Yellow
Are (gorillas) (bigger) than (rabbits)?

57

5 Food and drink

Look!

Guess What!

1 🎧 5.01 **Listen and point.**

2 🎧 5.02 **Listen, point, and repeat.**

3 🎧 5.03 **Listen and answer the questions.**

4 (Think) **Describe and guess who.**

He wants pasta for lunch.   Tom!

1 pasta
2 yogurt
3 soup
4 pizza
5 salad
6 nuts
7 tea
8 coffee
9 cookie
10 chips

5 **Listen and choose. Then sing the song.**

1 I always have a sandwich/pizza for lunch,
And I usually have some fruit.
Sometimes I have yogurt/soup,
But I never have cookies or chips.
No, he never has cookies or chips!

2 I usually have pasta/salad for dinner,
And sometimes I have some soup.
I always have some vegetables/fruit,
But I never have cookies or chips.
No, he never has cookies or chips!

He never has cookies or chips!

 6 (Think) **Look at the song. Then read and correct the sentences.**

1 I never have a sandwich for lunch.
2 I always have pasta for dinner.
3 Sometimes I have chips for lunch.
4 I never have vegetables for dinner.
5 I always have cookies for dinner.

Number 1. He always has a sandwich for lunch.

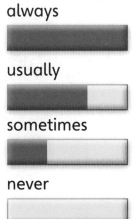

always

usually

sometimes

never

 7 (About Me) **Make sentences and say true or false.**

I always have chips for lunch.

False!

Remember!
I always have vegetables for dinner.
He never has cookies for dinner.

Grammar fun!

8 🎧 5.05 **Listen and repeat.**

How often do you have salad for lunch?

Every day.

Usually.

Sometimes.

Never.

9 (About Me) **Make questions. Then ask and answer with a friend.**

How often
do you
have

for breakfast?

for lunch?

for dinner?

10 **Tell the class about you and your friend.**

Pablo has toast for breakfast every day. I usually have yogurt.

11 🎧 5.06 **Go to page 103. Listen and repeat the chant.**

Remember

How often do you have vegetables for lunch?
Every day. Usually. Sometimes. Never.

Grammar fun!

       Grammar   → Workbook page 50

Skills: *Listening and speaking*

Let's start! **What do you usually have for lunch?**

12 **Listen and match.**

Grace

a

Monday	Tuesday	Wednesday	Thursday
pizza	pasta	soup	sandwich
salad	vegetables	salad	salad
fruit	yogurt	yogurt	fruit
yogurt	water	water	yogurt
water			water

Louis

b

Monday	Tuesday	Wednesday	Thursday
sandwich	chicken	soup	pasta
salad	salad	salad	vegetables
fruit	fruit	yogurt	fruit
yogurt	nuts	fruit	juice
water	juice	water	

13 **Listen again and answer the questions.**

1 How often does Grace have salad for lunch?
2 Does Grace sometimes have pizza?
3 How often does Louis have nuts?
4 Does Louis like yogurt?

14 **About Me** **Ask and answer with a friend.**

Do you always have a healthy lunch?
Do you usually have fruit, vegetables, or salad?
What do you never have for lunch?

Writing

 Workbook page 51: Make a lunch diary and write about it.

16   Listen and repeat. Then act.

tea   orange juice   pizza   cookies   chips   nuts

How much is the orange juice?

It's one dollar.

Can I have two, please?

Yes, of course.

How much are the cookies?

They're fifty cents.

Can I have three, please?

Yes, of course.

Say it!

17 Listen and repeat.

Aardvarks come out in the dark.

aardvark

Where does water come from?

1 🎧 5.11 **Listen and repeat.**

1. rain
2. glacier
3. well
4. spring

2 CLIL ▶ **Watch the video.**

3 **What can you see in the pictures?**

Guess What!

About 60% of our body is made up of water.

4 **Where are the big rivers in your country?**

Let's collaborate!

buy

OUR

sell

BUSINESS PLAN

count

think about

plan

use money

LEMONADE BAKE SALE

Cakes for Sale ☺

Look!

Guess What!

1 🎧 **Listen and point.**
   6.01

2 🎧 **Listen, point, and repeat.**
   6.02

3 🎧 **Listen and answer the questions.**
   6.03

4 🤔 **Describe and guess who.**

He has a cold.   Tom!

1 cold
2 cough
3 earache
4 stomachache
5 backache
6 sore throat
7 temperature
8 toothache
9 headache

5 🎧 6.04 **Listen and match. Then sing the song.**

1 Oh, dear, what's the matter?
What's the matter with you, Tim?
I have a headache.
Oh, dear, poor you!

2 Oh, dear, what's the matter?
What's the matter with Max?
He has a stomachache.
Oh, dear, poor him!

3 Oh, dear, what's the matter?
What's the matter with Mary?
She has a cough and a cold.
Oh, dear, poor her!

6 🎧 6.05 **Now listen and say the names.**

7 Think **Play a mime game.**

What's the matter with Charlie?

He has a stomachache.

Do you have a stomachache?

Yes, I do.

Remember

What's the matter?
I have a cough and a cold.

Grammar fun!

8 🎧 6.06 **Listen and repeat.**

Can you go sailing today?

No, I can't. I have a sore throat and a temperature.

9 🎧 6.07 **Listen and match.**

1   2   3   4

a   b   c   d

10 Think **Ask questions and say why you can't.**

Can you go ice-skating today?

No, I can't. I have an earache.

11 🎧 6.08 **Go to page 103. Listen and repeat the chant.**

Remember!

Can you play basketball today?
No, I can't. I have a cough and a cold.

Grammar fun!

Grammar

→ Workbook page 58

Skills: *Reading and speaking*

 Let's start! **How often do you have a cold?**

12 **Read and listen. Then match.**

Do you have a cold?

Make some lemon and honey! Lemon and honey is a very healthy drink. It's good for colds, and it's easy to make! Try this simple recipe at home.

1 You need a lemon, some honey, and some hot water.
2 Cut the lemon. Squeeze the juice into a cup.
3 Add some honey.
4 Add the hot water. Be careful! An adult can help.

It's ready! Now sit down and enjoy your lemon and honey!

13 **Read again and say *true* or *false*.**

1 Lemon and honey is a healthy drink.
2 It isn't good for colds.
3 It's difficult to make.
4 You need hot water for the drink.

14 **Ask and answer with a friend.**

What healthy foods and drinks can you make?
Can you make a salad?
Can you make a fruit salad?
Can you make orange juice?
Can you make a sandwich?

Writing

 Workbook page 59: Write a recipe for a healthy food or drink.

15 🎧 6.10 ▶ Story **Read and listen. Watch.**

1 Week 6
We need skateboards.

Let's ask our cousin Chris!

He goes to skateboarding club today.

2

3 Skateboarding competition today
Win a skateboard!

It's a competition!

Go, Chris!

4 Oh, dear!

Are you OK, Chris?

Yes, I think so. My leg hurts, but I'm OK. Don't worry.

5 Do you have a headache, Chris?

No, I'm OK now.

But where's your skateboard?

6 Skateboarding competition today
Win a skateboard!

Max!

He's really good!

7 That's OK! I'm good at skateboarding, but Max is very good!

Good job, Max!

Sorry, Chris!

74 | Value: Be a good sport

→ Workbook page 60

16   **Listen and repeat. Then act.**

backache   earache   headache   temperature   sore throat   cough

1

Are you OK?

Yes, I think so. Don't worry.

Oh, good!

2

Are you OK?

No, I don't think so. I have a headache.

Oh, dear!

Say it!

17  Listen and repeat.

Spiders spin special webs.

spider

What can we use plants for?

1 🎧 6.13 **Listen and repeat.**

1

fabric

2

fuel

3

medicine

2 CLIL ▶ **Watch the video.**

3 🎧 6.14 **Listen and say what picture it is.**

Guess! What! *Some bamboo plants can grow almost one meter in a day.*

1
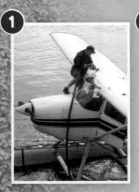

2

3

4

5

4 **Can you think of something new you could make from a plant?**

Let's collaborate!

OUR PLANT-BASED PRODUCT
review
create ask and answer
write persuade
brainstorm
PLANT-BASED OIL

Review Units 5 and 6

1 Find the words and match to the photographs.

pizzalpastapsaladesoup

2 🎧 6.15 Listen and say the names.

3 Read and say the names.

1 She likes making salad.
2 He sometimes makes pizza.
3 He likes making soup.
4 She often makes pasta with chicken and vegetables.

4 Make your own word puzzle for your friend.

Choose food or health:
toothachebcoughocold

Joe

Will

Rosie

Sara

→ Workbook pages 64–65

I never have pizza for breakfast!

How often do you have pasta for dinner? Every day.

7 Buildings

Look!

▶

Guess What!

1 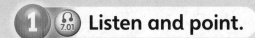 **Listen and point.**

2 (7.02) **Listen, point, and repeat.**

3 (7.03) **Listen and answer the questions.**

4 (Think) **Describe and guess where.**

There are lots of old toys here.

Attic!

1 first floor		**6** roof	
2 second floor		**7** basement	
3 third floor		**8** garage	
4 fourth floor		**9** stairs	
5 elevator		**10** attic	

5 (7.04) **Listen and choose. Then sing the song.**

1 Where were you yesterday?
Where were you yesterday morning?
I was in the kitchen/living room,
In my apartment on the third floor.

2 Where were you yesterday?
Where were you yesterday afternoon?
I was in the living room/bedroom,
In my apartment on the third floor.

3 Where were you yesterday?
Where were you yesterday evening?
I was in the roof garden/attic,
Above my apartment on the third floor.
My apartment on the third floor.
The third floor. The third floor.

6 (7.05) **Listen and say the names.**

John   Marta   Leon   Lola

7 (About Me) **Ask and answer with a friend.**

Where were you yesterday morning?

I was at home. I was in the living room.

Remember

Where were you yesterday
morning?
I was in the kitchen.

Grammar fun!

8 🎧 7.06 **Listen and repeat.**

Were you at home last night?

No, I wasn't. I was at the movies.

Yes, I was.

Were you at home?

9 (Think) **Make questions. Ask and answer with a friend.**

Questions

Were you	at home	yesterday morning?
	at school	yesterday afternoon?
	at the movies	yesterday evening?
	at a restaurant	last night?
	on the bus	
	in the hospital	
	at a shopping mall	
	at the swimming pool	

10 (About Me) **Play a guessing game.**

Were you in the hospital last night?

No, I wasn't. Guess again.

11 🎧 7.07 **Go to page 103. Listen and repeat the chant.**

Remember

Were you at home last night?
Yes, I was.   No, I wasn't.

Grammar fun!

Grammar

→ Workbook page 68

Skills: *Listening and speaking*

Let's start! **Who's your favorite singer?**

12 🎧 7.08 **Look at Misha's diary. Listen and choose.**

Misha

+

Saturday

<u>Morning</u>
at home / in a hotel / at a shopping mall

<u>Lunch</u>
in a restaurant / at home / at a park

<u>Afternoon</u>
at home / in the recording studio / at the movie theater

<u>Evening</u>
in a hotel / at home / at a concert

13 🎧 7.08 **Listen again and answer the questions.**

1 Where was Misha in the morning?
2 Where was she at lunch?
3 Where was she in the afternoon?
4 Where was she in the evening?

14 (About Me) **Ask and answer with a friend.**

Where were you on Saturday morning?
Where were you on Sunday afternoon?
Were you at the park on Saturday?
Were you at a concert on Saturday evening?

Writing

➡ Workbook page 69: Choose one day. Where were you? Write a diary for that day.

15 🎧 7.09 ▶ Story **Read and listen. Watch.**

Value: Take care of your possessions

→ Workbook page 70

16   **Listen and repeat. Then act.**

| Grandpa | Ben | Jane | Grandma | Lara | Uncle John |

1

Hello?

Hello, it's Sam. Is Jane there, please?

Yes, she is. Just a minute.

Thank you.

2

Hello?

Hello, it's Sally. Is Grandpa there, please?

No, I'm sorry, he isn't.

OK, thank you. Goodbye.

17 **Listen and repeat.**

Black ducks stand on rocks.

black duck

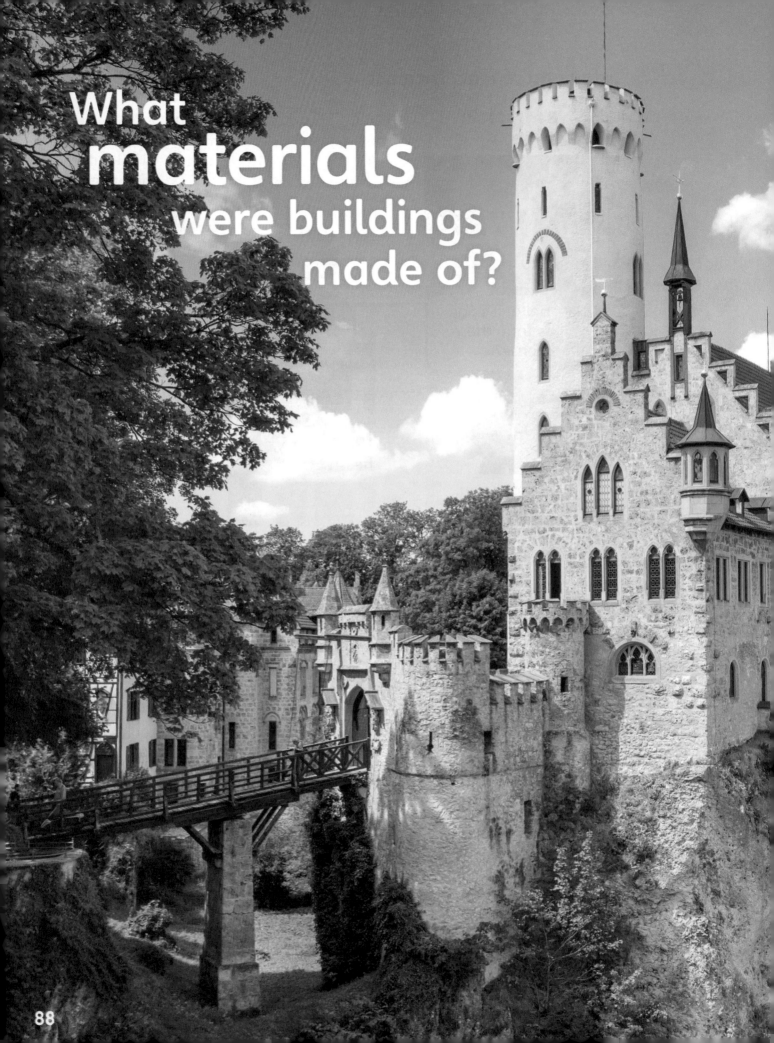

What materials were buildings made of?

1 🎧 **7.12 Listen and repeat.**

1 clay

2 stone

3 animal skins

2 CLIL ▶ **Watch the video.**

3 **What are these buildings made of?**

1

2

3

4

Guess What!
Animal skins were used for water bottles in the eighth century.

4 **What different things are made of stone?**

Let's collaborate!

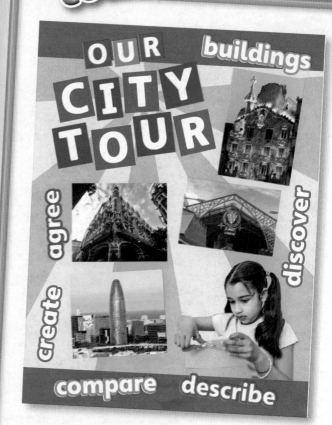

OUR CITY TOUR buildings

create agree compare describe discover

Look!

Guess What!

1 🎧 8.01 **Listen and point.**

2 🎧 8.02 **Listen, point, and repeat.**

Today's weather

Temperature

Weather

3 🎧 8.03 **Listen and say the numbers.**

4 (About Me) **Ask and answer with a friend.**

Do you like cold weather?   No, I don't. I like hot weather.

1 hot
2 sunny
3 cold
4 warm
5 snowy
6 cloudy
7 foggy
8 windy
9 rainy

5 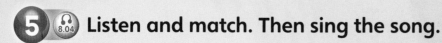 8.04 **Listen and match. Then sing the song.**

1 What was the weather like yesterday?
It was cold and rainy.
What's the weather like today?
It's hot and sunny.
Today it's hot and sunny.
So we can go out and play.
Hooray!

2 What was the weather like yesterday?
It was cold and foggy.
What's the weather like today?
It's cold and snowy.
Today it's cold and snowy.
So we can go out and play.
Hooray!

6 8.05 **Listen and answer the questions.**

yesterday morning · yesterday afternoon · yesterday evening · last night

7 Think **Ask and answer with a friend. Say *true* or *false*.**

What was the weather like yesterday?

It was cold and snowy.

False! It was cold and rainy.

Remember!
It was cold and rainy yesterday.
It's hot and sunny today.

Grammar fun!

8 (8.06) **Listen and repeat.**

1

Was it cloudy on Monday?

No, it wasn't. It was hot and sunny.

2

Was it rainy on Saturday?

Yes, it was.

9 (8.07) **Look at the weather diary. Listen and answer the questions.**

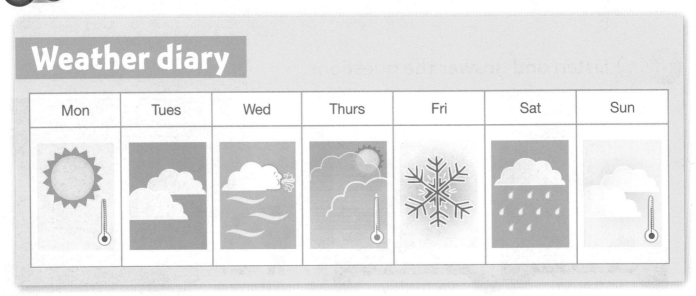

Weather diary

Mon	Tues	Wed	Thurs	Fri	Sat	Sun

10 (About Me) **Make a weather diary. Ask and answer with a friend.**

Was it hot and sunny on Saturday?

No, it wasn't. It was cold and rainy.

11 (8.08) **Go to page 103. Listen and repeat the chant.**

Remember

Was it hot and sunny on Monday?
Yes, it was.   No, it wasn't.

Grammar fun!

Grammar

→ Workbook page 76

Skills: *Reading and speaking*

Let's start! **Is it snowy in your country?**

12 🎧 8.09 **Read and listen. Then match.**

Hi Kalu,

1 How are you? I'm fine. It was my birthday on Saturday. I'm eleven now. My birthday was great. It was a cold and snowy day, and I was at the Sapporo Snow Festival with my family.

2 The snow festival is every year in February. It's fantastic. It's really big, and there are lots of amazing snow sculptures. This is a photograph of my favorite snow sculpture this year. Can you see what it is? It's a snow building.

3 There are also snow animals and lots of snowmen and snow women. This is a snow family!

4 The snow festival is beautiful at night, too. What's your favorite festival?

Email me soon.

Best wishes,

Yasuko

13 **Read and say *true* or *false*.**

1 Yasuko's birthday was on Sunday.
2 Yasuko was at the snow festival with her friends.
3 The snow festival is every April.
4 Yasuko likes the snow festival.
5 You can see lots of snow sculptures at the festival.

14 (About Me) **Ask and answer with a friend.**

When's your birthday?
What festivals do you have in your country?
What's your favorite festival?

Writing

→ Workbook page 77: Write about your favorite festival.

1 Adventure Playground

Good job, everyone!
Our Adventure Playground is ready!
Please come to the opening party
on Saturday at four o' clock.

2 It's Saturday today!

What time does the party start?

At four o'clock.

Good job, everyone!
Our Adventure Playground is ready!
Please come to the opening party
on Saturday at four o' clock.

Hurry up, we're late!

3 Adventure Playground

Welcome, everyone, and thank you for your hard work!

I want to be on TV!

4 The Adventure Playground is now open!

5 Wow! This is fantastic.

Faster!

Look! There's an owl.

Value: Work hard and try your best

→ Workbook page 78

16   **Listen and repeat. Then act.**

> TV program   talent show   movie   snow festival
> birthday party   swimming competition

1 When does the movie start?

At five o'clock.

Hurry up! We're late.

2 What time does the birthday party start?

OK, we have time.

At seven thirty.

Say it!

17   **Listen and repeat.**

Elands eat grass and are land animals.

eland

What's the weather like around the world?

1 🎧 8.13 **Listen and repeat.**

1
hurricane

2
tornado

3
rainstorm

4
blizzard

5
thunder and lightning

2 CLIL ▶ **Watch the video.**

3 **What's the weather like? Read and match.**

1 This weather's snowy and very cold.
2 It's a cone-shaped storm above the land.
3 This weather's cloudy and very rainy.
4 After we see this, it's very noisy.
5 It goes above the ocean, then on the land. It has an eye.

Guess What!
The middle of a hurricane is called its eye.

Let's collaborate!

4 **What kind of weather would you like to write about in a story?**

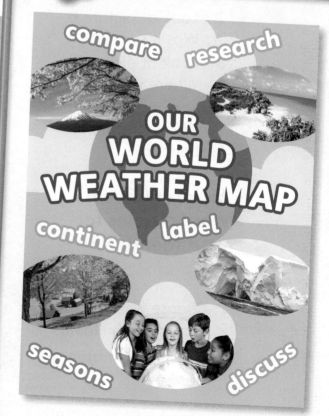
compare   research
OUR
WORLD
WEATHER MAP
continent   label
seasons   discuss

Review Units 7 and 8

1 Find the words and match to the photographs.

ysown

nusny

yiran

dinwy

2 🎧 8.14 **Listen and say the letters.**

3 Read and answer.

1 Look at picture a. What was the weather like?

2 Look at picture b. Was it sunny?

3 Look at picture c. Where was she?

4 Look at picture d. Was he at the beach?

4 Make your own word puzzles for your friend.

Choose weather or places in a building:
orof tiasrs mbtaense

→ Workbook pages 82–83

Yesterday at twelve thirty …

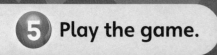

Mrs. Long

Lucy

Mr. Long

Miles

Player 1

1 Was it windy?
2 Was it hot?
3 Where was the cat?
4 Where was the gorilla?
5 Was the bike in the garage?
6 Was Lucy in the attic?

Player 2

1 Was it snowy?
2 Was it cold?
3 Where was the dog?
4 Where was the penguin?
5 Was the parrot in the kitchen?
6 Was Miles in the basement?

Chants

Welcome back! (page 8)

 Listen and repeat the chant.

Ten, twenty, thirty,
Forty, fifty, sixty,
Seventy, eighty, ninety,
And one hundred!
I can count to one hundred.

Ten, twenty, thirty,
Forty, fifty, sixty,
Seventy, eighty, ninety,
And one hundred!
I can count to one hundred.

Unit 1 (page 18)

 Listen and repeat the chant.

Are you good at skiing?
Yes, I am. Yes, I am.
What are you good at?
I'm good at skiing.

Are you good at ice-skating?
No, I'm not. No, I'm not.
What are you good at?
I'm good at roller-skating.

Unit 2 (page 28)

 Listen and repeat the chant.

Start at the traffic lights!
Go straight ahead.
Turn left at the bank.
Stop! Stop! Stop!

Start at the traffic lights!
Go straight ahead.
Turn right at the park.
Stop! Stop! Stop!

Unit 3 (page 40)

 Listen and repeat the chant.

What do you want to be?
I want to be a singer.
Do you want to be a singer?
Yes, I do. Yes, I do.

Do you want to be a teacher?
No, I don't. No, I don't.
I want to be a doctor.
George wants to be a doctor.

Unit 4 (page 50)

 Listen and repeat the chant.

Are giraffes taller than penguins?
Yes, they are. Yes, they are.
Are koalas noisier than bears?
No, they aren't. No, they aren't.

Are snakes longer than crocodiles?
Yes, they are. Yes, they are.
Are frogs bigger than owls?
No, they aren't. No, they aren't.

Unit 5 (page 62)

 Listen and repeat the chant.

How often do you have salad for lunch?
Every day. Every day.
I have salad for lunch every day.
He has salad for lunch every day.

How often do you have toast for breakfast?
Never. Never. Never.
I never have toast for breakfast.
She never has toast for breakfast.

Unit 6 (page 72)

 Listen and repeat the chant.

Can you go sailing today?
No, I can't. No, I can't.
I have a sore throat and a temperature.
Oh, dear! A sore throat and a temperature.

Can you play basketball today?
No, I can't. No, I can't.
I have a cough and a cold.
Oh, dear! A cough and a cold.

Unit 7 (page 84)

 Listen and repeat the chant.

Were you at home last night?
Yes, I was. Yes, I was.
I was at home.

Were you at home last night?
No, I wasn't. No, I wasn't.
I was at the movies.

Unit 8 (page 94)

 Listen and repeat the chant.

Was it hot and sunny on Monday?
Yes, it was. Yes, it was.
It was hot and sunny.

Was it hot and sunny on Tuesday?
No, it wasn't. No, it wasn't.
It was cloudy.

Acknowledgments

Many thanks to everyone in the excellent team at Cambridge University Press & Assessment in Spain, the UK, and India.

The authors and publishers would like to thank the following contributors:

Blooberry Design: concept design, cover design, book design
Hyphen: publishing management, page make-up
Ann Thomson: art direction
Gareth Boden: commissioned photography
Jon Barlow: commissioned photography
Ian Harker: class audio recording
John Marshall Media: "Grammar fun" recordings
Robert Lee, Dib Dib Dub Studios: song and chant composition
Vince Cross: theme tune composition
James Richardson: arrangement of theme tune
Phaebus: "CLIL" video production
Kiki Foster: "Look!" video production
Bill Smith Group: "Grammar fun" and story animations
Sounds Like Mike Ltd: "Grammar Fun" video production

The authors and publishers acknowledge the following sources of copyright material and are grateful for the permissions granted. While every effort has been made, it has not always been possible to identify the sources of all the material used, or to trace all copyright holders. If any omissions are brought to our notice, we will be happy to include the appropriate acknowledgements on reprinting and in the next update to the digital edition, as applicable.

Key: U = Unit, Emt = End matter

Photography

The following images are sourced from Getty Images:

U0: Somsak Bumroongwong/EyeEm; FG Trade/E+; Cimmerian/E+; Jose Luis Pelaez Inc/DigitalVision; kyoshino/E+; exxorian/DigitalVision Vectors; Westend61; Gerardo Ricardo López/Moment Open; JohnnyGreig/iStock/Getty Images Plus; Monashee Frantz/OJO Images; sad444/iStock/Getty Images Plus; Imgorthand/E+; Daniel A. Leifheit/Moment; Denis Dumoulin/500px; JBryson/iStock/Getty Images Plus; subjob/ iStock/Getty Images Plus; David Kenny/iStock/Getty Images Plus; U1: Daniel Milchev/ The Image Bank; mbbirdy/E+; Sebastian Condrea/Moment; Imgorthand/E+; Portra/ DigitalVision; Ascent Xmedia/Stone; Sean Justice/The Image Bank; Nikoncharly/ iStock/Getty Images Plus; Digital Vision/Photodisc; David Cayless; David Kenny/ iStock/Getty Images Plus; Arianna Tarenzi/EyeEm; perkmeup/iStock/Getty Images Plus; J and J Productions/Photodisc; Chris Stein/ DigitalVision; Michi B; U2: Katsumi Murouchi/Moment; frytka/E+; Tom Werner/ DigitalVision; anilyanik/DigitalVision Vectors; Jasenka Arbanas/Moment; Richard Sharrocks/Moment; NurPhoto; Jeremy Walker/Stone; leonmoran/iStock/Getty Images Plus; mihtiander/iStock/Getty Images Plus; Mauricio Handler/Photodisc; View Pictures/Universal Images Group; Michael DeYoung/Tetra images; U3: Morsa Images/DigitalVision; Digital Vision/Photodisc; FatCamera/E+; Pawita Warasiri/EyeEm; Nathan Bilow/Photodisc; Simon GRATIEN/ Moment; GABRIEL BOUYS/AFP; fototrav/E+; Klaus Vedfelt/DigitalVision; mihtiander/ iStock/Getty Images Plus; RainervonBrandis/E+; Philip Dumas/Moment; Maskot; Leonardo Laschera/EyeEm; rusm/iStock/Getty Images Plus; MLADEN ANTONOV/ AFP; U4: letty17/E+; Biswadip Ghosh/500px; Ekaterina Goncharova/Moment; Lezh/ E+; Foodcollection; Alistair Berg/Stone; Frans Lemmens/Corbis Unreleased; UpperCut Images; CreativeNature_nl/iStock/Getty Images Plus; Mike Powles/ Stone; Oli Scarff/Getty Images News; jordieasy/iStock/Getty Images Plus; Marianne Purdie/ Moment; QueGar3/iStock/Getty Images Plus; szefei/iStock/ Getty Images Plus; annick vanderschelden photography/Moment; C Flanigan/ FilmMagic; Hugo Ortu±o Suárez/ Moment; 1001nights/E+; U5: Roberto A Sanchez/E+; pagadesign/E+; twomeows/ Moment; Ivan Negru/500px; Carbonero Stock/Moment; Image Source; rudisill/ E+; clubfoto/iStock/Getty Images Plus; Weekend Images Inc./iStock/Getty Images Plus; David Papazian/Corbis; David Cayless; AB Photography/iStock/Getty Images Plus; Paul Souders/Stone; Roberto Moiola/Sysaworld/Moment; somnuk krobkum/ Moment; energyy/iStock/Getty Images Plus; U6: trigga/E+; GYRO PHOTOGRAPHY/ amana images; Paolo Negri/Photographer's Choice; Jacky Parker Photography/ Moment; Ekaterina Goncharova/Moment; Eskay Lim/EyeEm; enjoynz/DigitalVision Vectors; Andersen Ross Photography Inc/DigitalVision; Catherine Falls Commercial/ Moment; Fabrice LEROUGE/ONOKY; BSIP/Collection Mix: Subjects; chameleonseye/ iStock/Getty Images Plus; Klaus Vedfelt/DigitalVision; szefei/iStock/Getty Images Plus; jokuephotography/iStock/Getty Images Plus; John Elk III/The Image Bank Unreleased; Westend61; Andersen Ross/Photodisc; Luca Silvestro Santilli/EyeEm; Paul Viant/iStock/Getty Images Plus; U7: Shaun Egan/The Image Bank; MOF/E+; Cultura Exclusive/Quim Roser/Image Source; Â©fitopardo/ Moment; FOTOGRAFIA INC./E+; Coal Photography/Alexander Legaree/ Moment; Jupiterimages/Stockbyte; kali9/iStock/Getty Images Plus; Birgid Allig/ Corbis; Daniel A. Leifheit/Moment; KathyKafka/iStock/Getty Images Plus; imetlion/iStock/Getty Images Plus; U8: Peerakit JIrachetthakun/Moment; Buena Vista Images/Photodisc; Ron and Patty Thomas/E+; Jack Pan/500px/500Px Plus; moodboard/Brand X Pictures; Ron Evans/ Stockbyte; Sungmoon Han/ EyeEm; Wang Zhaobo/VCG; YOSHIKAZU TSUNO/ Gamma-Rapho; wisarut_ch/ Shutterstock; anmbph/iStock/Getty Images Plus; Wan Ru Chen/Moment; Warren Faidley/The Image Bank; Cultura RM Exclusive/Jason Persoff Stormdoctor/ Image Source; Manuel Peric/EyeEm; V_Sot/iStock/Getty Images Plus; John Sirlin/ EyeEm; Aaron Horowitz/The Image Bank; Alistair Berg/DigitalVision; Stockbyte; benedektibor/iStock/Getty Images Plus.

The following images are sourced from other libraries:

U0: Tatiana Popova/Shutterstock; View Stock/Alamy; Bejim/Shutterstock; ESB Professional/Shutterstock; Kuttig - People/Alamy Stock Photo; Image navi - Sozaijiten/ Alamy; Thierry GRUN/Alamy; Daniela Pelazza/Shutterstock; MT511/ Shutterstock; irin-k/Shutterstock; Moiz Husein Dossaji/Shutterstock; Jirik V/ Shutterstock; U1: Pakhnyushchy/Shutterstock; Lora liu/Shutterstock; Mira/ Alamy; Image Source Plus/Alamy; Radius Images/Design Pics/Alamy; Amy Myers/ Shutterstock; David & Micha Sheldon/F1online digitale Bildagentur GmbH/ Alamy; U2: QQ7/Shutterstock; Greg Williams/Shutterstock; Michael Kemp/ Alamy; yuanyuan xie/Zoonar GmbH/ Alamy; Dan Kosmayer/Shutterstock; Laborant/Shutterstock; gmstockstudio/ Shutterstock; popartic/Shutterstock; KULISH VIKTORIIA/Shutterstock; Joseph Sohm/ Shutterstock; Elnur Amikishiyev/ Shutterstock; Sergio Bertino/Shutterstock; Styve Reineck/Shutterstock; Denis Radovanovic/Shutterstock; tab62/Shutterstock; U3: StockLite/Shutterstock; Juice Images272/Alamy; V.S.Anandhakrishna/Shutterstock; Belikova Oksana/ Shutterstock; Lumi images/Alamy; lunamarina/Shutterstock; Monkey Business Images/Shutterstock; Grzegorz Petrykowski/Shutterstock; Leandro Mise/ Alamy; Lloyd Sutton/Alamy; Steve Arnold/Alamy; U4: Milosz Maslanka/ Shutterstock; JI de Wet/Shutterstock; Ryan M. Bolton/Shutterstock; Anton_ Ivanov/ Shutterstock; Subbotina Anna/Shutterstock; Media Home/Shutterstock; Cathy Keifer/ Shutterstock; Ricardo Canino/Shutterstock; Johan Swanepoel/ Shutterstock; subin pumsom/Shutterstock; paytai/Shutterstock; Matt Jeppson/ Shutterstock; reptiles4all/ Shutterstock; Bill Kennedy/Shutterstock; Dirk Ercken/ Shutterstock; Audrey Snider- Bell/Shutterstock; Mikadun/Shutterstock; Jean-Edouard Rozey/Shutterstock; Jim Pickerell/Stock Connection Blue/Alamy; U5: Nitr/Shutterstock; triocean/Shutterstock; page frederique/Shutterstock; M. Unal Ozmen/Shutterstock; Lestertair/Shutterstock; Africa Studio/Shutterstock; papkin/Shutterstock; Alessio Orru/Shutterstock; Reika/Shutterstock; Suprun Vitaly/Shutterstock; nito/Shutterstock; Marina Grau/ Shutterstock; the stock company/Shutterstock; sondem/Shutterstock; Gerhard Zwerger-Schoner/ imageBROKER.com GmbH & Co. KG/Alamy; Stephen Coyne/ Art Directors/ Alamy; Denis Kichatof/Shutterstock; peresanz/Shutterstock; U6: Bob Mitchell/ Corbis; Radius Images/Design Pics/Alamy; Irina Mos/Shutterstock; Malivan_ luliia/Shutterstock; Lifestyle Travel Photo/Shutterstock; Destinyweddingstudio/ Shutterstock; Mikhail Pozhenko/Shutterstock; Denis Tabler/Shutterstock; tristan tan/ Shutterstock; Russel Wasserfall/Gallo Images/Alamy; Antonova Ganna/ Shutterstock; Elly Godfroy/Alamy; Alexandr Makarov/Shutterstock; Africa Studio/Shutterstock; my nordic/Shutterstock; U7: Gallo Images - LKIS/Alamy; Khakimullin Aleksandr/ Shutterstock; Monkey Business Images/Shutterstock; Christian Mueller/Shutterstock; balabolka/Shutterstock; Andre Babiak/Alamy; dwphotos/Shutterstock; Sasa Komlen/ Shutterstock; MORANDI Bruno/hemis. fr/Alamy; Pecold/Shutterstock; Ragnar Th Sigurdsson/ARCTIC IMAGES/Alamy; saras66/Shutterstock; kosmos111/Shutterstock; David South/Alamy; U8: Robert Postma/All Canada Photos/Alamy; icollection/Alamy; Cal Vornberger/ Alamy; nodff/Shutterstock; stock_shot/Shutterstock; wisarut_ch/ Shutterstock; peresanz/Shutterstock; Jim Reed/Jim Reed Photography - Severe&/ Corbis; Gregory Pelt/Shutterstock; Igumnova Irina/Shutterstock; Adrian Sherratt/ Alamy; blue67design/Shutterstock; Elena Schweitzer/Shutterstock.

Front Cover photography by Roman Pretot/500px.

Illustrations

A Corazon Abierto (Sylvie Poggio Artists); Luke Newell; Marcus Cutler (Sylvie Poggio Artists); Pablo Gallego.